How To
REACH
Your
FRIENDS
for
CHRIST

Elmer Towns

1-800-553-GROW (4769)

Ephesians Four Ministries
CHURCH GROWTH INSTITUTE
P.O. Box 7, Elkton, MD 21922-0007
ORDERS: PO Box 9176, Oxnard, CA 93031-9176

First Printing, February 1989
Second Printing, August 1990
Third Printing, May 1994
Fourth Printing, November 1995
Fifth Printing, April 1997
Sixth Printing, February 1999
Seventh Printing, May 2007
Copyright © 1989 Church Growth Institute
Forest, Virginia, USA
All Rights Reserved
Printed in the United States of America
ISBN: 0-941005-14-3

CONTENTS

123 333

INTRODUCTION

Every Christian knows someone who is not a Christian. Some of these persons are our close friends. We should share our faith with them, but we usually don't. Sometimes the problem is internal, we are fearful or we are intimidated. Other times the problem is one of methodology; we don't know how to reach them.

This book is written to help you influence your friends to become Christians. Yet, this is not a typical soulwinning book. It has a different approach than most books on personal evangelism. It shows how the average Christian can draw his or her friends closer to salvation without actually attempting to get them to make a decision to be saved. The book is not written for you to use to preach to your friends or to tell you how to get them to make a decision. Instead, this book is about influencing your friends for Christ or stairstepping them to Him.

The first chapter describes wrong attitudes many Christians have about witnessing to their friends and presents the biblical position of influencing or stairstepping friends to Jesus Christ. It shows how Andrew told his brother Peter about Jesus Christ. The second chapter suggests the attitude you will need to stairstep friends to Jesus Christ. The third chapter looks at methods for moving your friends to Him. The final chapter suggests how to invite them to church.

Inviting friends to church is something that everyone can do, but very few do it. Christians should network their friends into the church so they are bonded to the local body of Jesus Christ. However, soulwinning has taken on such an eternal magnitude that most Christians say, "I can't do it." But this book will make stairstepping your friends to Christ so simple that you will respond, "I can do it." May God bless you as you do.

Elmer L. Towns
Lynchburg, Virginia

CHAPTER ONE

STAIRSTEPPING YOUR FRIENDS TO CHRIST

Cathy is a typical young all-American girl who married the man of her dreams. Both she and her husband work full time to achieve their goals. Cathy believed in God, was moral in character, and was involved in community activities. As a young girl she had made a salvation decision, but as she grew into young adulthood she forgot her commitment to Christ.

My wife, Ruth, worked in the same office with Cathy and tried to influence her for Christ. She didn't want to press Cathy prematurely, but she did want to help her spiritually. My wife did not try to preach to Cathy for several reasons. First, Cathy was not ready to enter into a relationship with a local church. Second, she knew some of the terminology, but didn't understand the meaning of Christian words. Finally, several physical barriers kept her from attending our church. Parking is hard to find and getting a good seat is difficult also. In addition, our church seats 4,000, and Cathy preferred to attend a small, family church.

Cathy had heard preaching over television but had not responded. Several strangers had invited her to attend their churches, but she declined. Her resistance broke down when Heritage Baptist Church in Lynchburg, Virginia, had a Friend Day in November 1981. I was the speaker as well as the friend invited by Rod Kidd, pastor at that time. When I told my wife about the idea of everyone inviting a friend, she thought of Cathy.

Ruth asked Cathy to attend church as her friend. Cathy agreed enthusiastically. The church was in her neighborhood, but she never would have attended by herself. At the service Ruth and Cathy sat together, and during the Friendship Hour, Ruth stood and introduced Cathy to the congregation.

After I preached, I gave an invitation for people to come forward where someone would pray with them to receive Christ. Twelve came forward, but Cathy did not respond. Perhaps the idea of publicly walking forward was new to her. Maybe she was scared, or perhaps she just wasn't ready. At any rate, that was her first exposure to gospel preaching, and she wasn't comfortable with it.

Sunday afternoon, Pastor Kidd wrote a letter to Cathy, offering pastoral help and friendship. He had planned to phone and visit all the Friend Day visitors, but the response was so great (from an average of 83 in attendance the church jumped that day to 237), that he couldn't personally phone or call on every visitor. Therefore, his wife made the phone calls. She contacted Cathy and offered friendship and help.

Monday night, one day after Cathy attended church, Pastor Kidd visited her home, and she and her husband recommitted their lives to Christ. The following week they went forward in the church service and publicly acknowledged their commitment.

WRONG ATTITUDES ABOUT REACHING YOUR FRIENDS

Every Christian has a "Cathy" in his or her life, but we create barriers that keep us from effectively influencing them. Following are four wrong attitudes that keep Christians from effectively reaching their friends for Christ.

1. *Christians are decision-oriented rather than discipleship-oriented.* Many Christians are so concerned about getting their friends to bow their heads and make a decision for Christ that they don't first prepare the hearts of their friends. They put emphasis on the result, rather than on conditions that will lead to the result. Because they are so decision-oriented, they create two barriers. First, some Christians push their friends to make a decision before they are ready. If the friends refuse, they have destroyed their relationship with them. Second, some Christians shy away from witnessing to their friends because they have been taught that soulwinning is getting a person to "sign on the bottom line," and they are uncomfortable with pressing decisions on others. However, you should think of winning your friends to Christ by influencing them in three steps:

1. Pre-conversion: witnessing

2. Conversion: accepting Christ

3. Post-conversion: Christian growth

This book focuses on the first step, witnessing. You can influence your friends to receive Christ by witnessing to them: "Ye shall be my witnesses" (Acts 1:8). Witnessing is sharing your faith with your friends, but does not necessarily include leading them through the plan of salvation. Witnessing is sharing what you have seen, what you have heard, and what you have experienced. You can tell your friends how much you enjoy hymn singing or what the Lord has done for you, yet not push them to get saved. Witnessing is putting salt on their tongues and making them thirsty for the Water of Life.

Because friends share things with friends, you should share your faith with your unsaved friends. This is pre-conversion witnessing.

When a Christian does something for a friend, especially if it is in the name of Jesus, it may not win the friend to Christ, but it may soften his or her heart to the Gospel. Every conversation you have with your friend about Christianity and every time you relate a Christian experience can actually move them closer to Jesus Christ. Just being with your friends makes them comfortable with you, and hopefully, comfortable with your Christian faith.

When you stairstep someone to salvation, they move first from a negative rejection of Christ to a neutral position. Then they move to a positive belief in Christ. They move from being a "God-hater" to being one who loves God.

Stages of Receptivity toward Christ

Rejection					Reception				
-5	-4	-3	-2	-1	+1	+2	+3	+4	+5

Stairstepping is using the natural relationship of friendship to influence a friend to Christ. You can positively influence your friends for Christ without arm-twisting or going out of your way to give them a tract. Just being a friend and talking about your faith moves them up the stair closer to salvation.

2. *Christians expect abnormal rather than normal responses.* Because of the sensational stories told in the pulpit, the average lay person is intimidated about soulwinning. One evangelist told this story: "When I went to the front door and asked the person if he was saved, he reached for a gun." This sensational story electrifies an audience, but the average Christian never meets a person with a gun in his hand. Because of these extreme stories, some Christians are afraid of abnormal or threatening responses. Others are afraid of bitter hostility when they witness, such as being cursed. And some expect people to fall to their knees in repentance or break down in tears. Since most laymen do not think that they can get such results, they keep quiet and do not share their faith.

Witnessing should be natural. Witnessing happens when two friends have coffee: the Christian talks about his church and shares what Christ means to him. Witnessing happens when two friends bowl: the Christian shares how he has overcome temptation since he has been saved. The credibility of the Christian is reinforced because his friend knows what used to defeat him. Witnessing happens when two friends go to the ball game: the Christian talks about how much he enjoys singing and worshipping the Lord at his church.

Witnessing should be as normal as friendship. For example, the checkout clerk at K-Mart shares the Gospel with her friend during lunch. Even if she doesn't try to win her friend to Christ, she can move her closer to salvation. She can stairstep her closer to the kingdom.

3. *Christians think evangelism should focus primarily on strangers rather than friends.* Often we hear the story of witnessing on an airplane to strangers. We think that an airplane is the place to win souls. Some Christians go on a Gospel team to the inner city to witness at a rescue mission. It may be easier to wit-

ness to those you will never see again, but your most effective influence is with your friends. You ought to witness to your friends and relatives because you have greater influence on them than on anyone else. The majority of New Testament evangelism was centered on witnessing to friends and relatives. Since you have already established a relationship with your friends, you should naturally use that bridge to share Jesus Christ.

4. *Christians have been motivated to evangelize by guilt rather than by love.* Quite often Christians are challenged to go witnessing during an evangelistic outreach of their church. Most of those who become involved feel good about it. But some do it out of guilt, and they don't feel good about their evangelism. And what about those who don't witness at all? They are told that they have disobeyed God, or that they have sinned by not giving out the Gospel. Guilt is heaped upon them. Those who load others down with guilt usually think they are motivating them to good works, as when some pastors use negative motivation to get positive results. They say, "If you are not a soul-winner, then you are not in the will of God." Guilt motivation is counterproductive. Rather than doing more, Christians feel guilty and do less. Using guilt to motivate a person to share his faith actually puts up barriers against evangelism.

Friends love their friends. Effective witnessing ought to be motivated by love. It is the most natural thing for a friend to give good news to his buddies. When friends talk, they talk about the good things that happen to them. They talk about how to improve their bowling or where the good sales are found. They may also share how they received Christ as their Saviour. Love is much more effective than guilt in getting friends to talk about Jesus.

ANDREW STAIRSTEPPED HIS BROTHER TO JESUS

Andrew was given the name "first called" because when Jesus began calling His disciples, Andrew was the first one called. A study of the first-called disciple indicates that he was not known for his preaching, teaching, or other communicating skills. His gift was bringing people to Jesus. He stairstepped people to the Saviour.

Andrew was a disciple of John the Baptist when John was baptizing in the Jordan River and the multitudes gathered to hear him preach. Another of the Baptist's disciples was young John (later known as John the beloved disciple). As disciples of John the Baptist, Andrew and John prepared candidates for baptism and gave directions to the multitude. They also taught young converts and answered questions.

An electrifying scene took place when Jesus appeared on the banks of the Jordan to be baptized: "The next day John seeth Jesus coming unto him, and saith, Behold the Lamb of God, which taketh away the sin of the world" (John 1:29). This was probably Andrew's introduction to Jesus Christ, the Messiah. Andrew heard a voice from heaven saying, "This is my beloved Son, in whom I am well pleased" (Matthew 3:17). Andrew also saw the Holy Spirit descending as a dove from heaven upon the Son of God (Matthew 3:16). Later the other young man, John, testified about this scene. He wrote, "And I saw, and bare record that this is the Son of God" (John 1:34).

Andrew and John followed Jesus when He left the river bank. It is not clear whether they were following Him at this time to become His disciples or just to learn more from him.

"What seek ye?" Jesus said to them (John 1:38). The two young men recognized that Jesus was a great teacher and asked where He was living.

"Come and see," Jesus answered (John 1:39).

The two followed Jesus home that evening. It was about 4:00 p.m. (the tenth hour) when they met Him (John 1:39). During that evening conversation, their questions were probably answered. Young Andrew came to realize that Jesus Christ was the promised Messiah. Because this is what Andrew told his brother the next day, it must have been part of the conversation that evening. How long they talked is not stated, but much can be discussed from 4:00 p.m. in the afternoon until the late evening hours.

The next day young Andrew found his brother Peter, described as, "He first findeth his own brother Simon" (John 1:41). The word *findeth* implies that Andrew had to search for Peter. Perhaps he looked at their home and then down by the boats. When he couldn't find Peter, he kept searching until he located him. When you attempt to reach your friends for Christ, you can't always wait until a convenient moment to share your faith with them. Sometimes you have to make an appointment, or do even as Andrew did, seek them out. Stairstepping may be casual, but it is not unintentional. Sometimes you must seek the opportunity to share your Christian experience with your friends.

The text indicates of Andrew, "He first findeth his own brother" (John 1:41), implying that Andrew found his brother Peter before John (actually second in sequence) found his brother James. The word first means "first before another" and not the first thing in his priority. This word speaks about our responsiveness to Jesus Christ. When Andrew heard the message and was convinced, he immediately went to tell his brother Peter about Jesus. Note, he did not need to take a class in evangelism, nor did he need to learn the plan of salvation. He simply shared with his brother what he knew about Jesus Christ. Stairstepping is sharing what is on your heart, not necessarily presenting a memorized formula for salvation. (The formula is not wrong, but there are times and places that it is not appropriate.)

Andrew was convinced that Jesus was the predicted Messiah because he told his brother, "We have found the Messias, which is, being interpreted, the Christ" (John 1:41). The word *Christ* is the Greek translation of the Hebrew word *anointed* or *Messiah*. The message of Jesus Christ changed Andrew's life.

The first illustration of Jesus' influence on a disciple's life had to do with friendship evangelism. Jesus' disciples did not first go out to preach publicly; they went out to influence their friends and relatives. They stairstepped them to faith in Christ. John reached his brother James, and Andrew reached Peter: "And he brought him to Jesus" (John 1:42). The word *brought* implies that Andrew had to overcome some resistance in Peter. Andrew's brother did not eagerly come to Jesus. Your friends do not always want to know about Jesus Christ, nor do they want to come to church. It takes persistence and commitment to reach your friends for Christ. Stairstepping is natural and effective, but it is not always easy.

EVANGELISM IS A PROCESS LEADING TO AN EVENT

Andrew is seen working two aspects of evangelism. First, he brings his brother to Jesus Christ. This is the process of evangelism that is called stairstepping a friend to Christ. Second, the event of conversion took place "when Jesus beheld him" (John 1:42). It takes the process of witnessing or stairstepping to lead a person to the event of salvation. Some who are effective at influencing a person actually may not be able to lead their friend to Christ. So those who are not able to lead a friend in praying the sinner's prayer should at least do what they are able to do. They should emphasize stairstepping their friends to Christ.

Salvation is illustrated by the birth of a baby. When a baby leaves his mother's womb and enters the world, he experiences his first birth. When a person is born into God's family, he experiences a second birth. Jesus described the new birth experience by saying, "Except a man be born again, he cannot see the kingdom of God" (John 3:3). Even though a baby is born at a specific hour, nine months elapse between conception and birth. The birth of the baby is like the event of salvation, and the nine-month gestation period is like stairstepping a person to Christ.

A birth certificate will state, "born alive at 1:15 a.m." A birth happens at a point in time; it is an event. The birth certificate will never read "born between 6:40 a.m. and 2:20 p.m." Even though labor may be long and hard, there is a point in time when the doctor slaps the baby and he begins to breathe independently from the mother. Nine months of prenatal development is the influence you exert on your friends to prepare them for the event called conversion or regeneration.

Each contact you make with your friend should move them closer to Jesus Christ. You may not be able to get them to pray to receive Christ the first time you share your faith or the ninth time you witness to them. However, you must have assurance that God is working in their heart and moving them toward the event of salvation. The process of stairstepping is sometimes called "pre-evangelism" or "pre-conversion." Sometimes stairstepping takes only a few hours, as when a person attends a Gospel meeting, hears the Gospel, and becomes converted during the invitation. At other times stairstepping takes years.

When Andrew went to tell his brother Peter about Jesus, the Bible says, "He first findeth his own brother Simon" (John 1:41). This implies that Andrew had a relationship with and knowledge of his brother. Finding your friend is part of pre-conversion stairstepping. After Andrew found Peter, "he brought him to Jesus" (John 1:42). This implies using a relationship for friendship evangelism. Perhaps as young boys, Andrew and Peter had discussed the coming Messiah. Perhaps they had discussed the national redemption of Israel and God visiting earth through the coming Christ. Andrew was able to build on this past relationship and announce to his brother, "We have found the Messias" (John 1:41).

REACHING YOUR FRIENDS IS THE WILL OF GOD

The will of God is that no one be lost (2 Peter 3:9). When you influence your friends for salvation, you are doing the work of evangelism and the will of God. For you to accomplish this work, you must first give yourself to Him: "But yield yourselves unto God, as those that are alive from the dead, and your members as instruments of righteousness unto God" (Romans 6:13). If you are going to attract others to Christ, you must radiate the peace and joy that only He can give.

CONCLUSION

Research indicates that most people who visit Sunday School are looking for friends, or they were brought by a friend. Research also shows that 86 percent of Christians indicate that the primary influence that brought them to Christ was a friend or relative. Stairstepping our friends to Christ is one of the most effective means of evangelism available to the contemporary church.

CHAPTER TWO

RIGHT ATTITUDES FOR STAIRSTEPPING YOUR FRIENDS TO CHRIST

Right attitudes will give you direction as you try to win your friends to Christ. Right attitudes involve right concern, right motives, and right sensitivity. You need them to win a friend to Christ. But right attitudes also involve saying the right thing at the right time. Ultimately, stairstepping your friends to Christ involves using right methods and following a right strategy.

Formula for Successful Stairstepping:

Right attitudes plus right actions = Success

Definitions:

Right Attitudes = Right thinking about a situation

Right Actions = Doing the right things about a situation

This chapter will answer the questions "Are you qualified?" and "Are you equipped?" Having the right attitudes will give you the right answers to these questions.

ARE YOU QUALIFIED?

1. *You must be born again.* For you to reach your friends for Jesus Christ, you must know Him yourself. It has been said that you can't give the measles unless you have the measles. You can't influence people to salvation unless you have experienced eternal life (1 John 5:12-13). When you have been born again (John 3:3-7) and have a personal realization of the love of God, you will want to share that with your friends.

2. *You must yield yourself to God.* If you would win your friends to Jesus Christ, you must make an active dedication of your life to Christ. First, you yield yourself "once and for all" in a commitment of your life to Jesus Christ: "But yield yourselves unto God" (Romans 6:13). Sometimes this is done by going forward in a Gospel service and making a public commitment of yourself to God.

Teenagers do this at campfires or in youth services. Such commitments do not have to be made publicly, but a public commitment usually is more effective. Then you must make a daily commitment of your life to God for a more effective witness. If you want to attract your friends to Christ, you must radiate the peace and joy that only Jesus Christ can give.

3. *You must realize that your friends outside of Christ are lost.* The will of God is that no one be lost (2 Peter 3:9). When you influence your friends for salvation, you are doing the will of God. Your friends may not be morally upstanding, or they may be as "solid as a rock" when it comes to character or stability. But if they have not prayed to receive Christ, they need to be saved.

You will not try to get your friends saved until you realize they are lost. So a right biblical attitude about their spiritual condition is necessary preparation for stairstepping them to salvation. First you must realize that your friends must be born again (John 3:3, 7). They are not saved if they have not called on the name of Christ.

Second, you must realize that your friends are not good enough to go to heaven: "There is none righteous, no, not one" (Romans 3:10). Many times you look at your friends through the eyes of your relationship. You like their laughter and enjoy their companionship. Because of your joy, it is sometimes difficult to see them as God sees them. But they are lost: "For all have sinned, and come short of the glory of God" (Romans 3:23).

You must be completely convinced that your friends' deepest spiritual need is salvation. Without such a conviction, any attempt to stairstep them to salvation will flounder and become a half-hearted effort of talking about religion. You must be convinced that every one of your friends will be lost eternally if they do not receive Jesus Christ as Savior (Romans 3:23, 5:12). When you begin to stairstep your friends to salvation, you must be convinced that Jesus can meet their deepest spiritual needs and that He is the only Savior from sin and the only way to heaven (John 14:6, Acts 4:12). When you have this conviction in your heart, it will influence your relationship with your friends, and you will want to share the Gospel with them.

4. *You must realize that stairstepping is biblical.* A few ministers have criticized those who invite their friends to church. These ministers believe that everyone must be a soulwinner and attempt to lead others to a salvation decision. As a result, when some Christians invite their friends to church, they think they are doing a lesser job for God, or they see themselves compromising their evangelistic outreach. How sad! Some Christians are evangelists (Ephesians 4:11) and can lead people to decisions. Others are used of God to be a witness or bring friends to church.

The method of stairstepping friends to Christ is found throughout the New Testament. Those who came to salvation wanted to share it with their family and friends. Jesus told the maniac of Gadara, "Go home to thy friends, and tell them how great things the Lord hath done for thee, and hath had compassion on thee" (Mark 5:19). Here was a new believer who immediately went to family and friends to share his lifechanging experience. When Zacchaeus came to know Christ, Jesus said, "This day is salvation come to this house" (Luke 19:9), implying that not only Zacchaeus, but his whole family should know about his changed life. When Cornelius was seeking salvation, the Bible describes it thusly, "And Cornelius waited for them (Peter and the brethren from Joppa), and had called together his kinsmen and near friends" (Acts 10:24). Cornelius told Peter, "Now therefore are we all here present before God, to hear all things that are commanded thee of God" (Acts 10:33). Cornelius brought his family and friends to hear the Gospel message. This is the same as inviting people to church.

When Paul prayed in prison, God sent an earthquake to release him. The Philippian jailer cried out in fear because he thought he had lost his prisoners, and hence his life. Paul and Silas witnessed to him and said, "Believe on the Lord Jesus Christ, and thou shalt be saved, and thy house" (Acts 16:31). The phrase, "and thy house," does not mean that the jailer's family would be saved automatically because he believed in Jesus Christ. It means that if his family believed as the jailer was challenged to do, the family would be saved. The result was that "When he had brought them into his house, he set meat before them, and rejoiced, believing in God with all his house" (Acts 16:34). The jailer not only came to know Jesus Christ, he made it possible for his family and friends to hear the message and get saved.

ARE YOU EQUIPPED?

You must have some basic equipment to stairstep your friends to Christ. Just as a carpenter has basic tools to help him or he cannot do the job adequately, so you need some basic things to influence your friends.

1. *You must know the Word of God.* Your life is the only Bible that your unsaved friends may ever read. Therefore, if you know the Bible and live by the Bible, it can influence their lives. God uses His word to convict of sin. The Christians at Thessalonica were examples for Jesus Christ: "So that ye were ensamples to all that believe in Macedonia and Achaia. For from you sounded out the word of the Lord not only in Macedonia and Achaia, but also in every place your faith to God-ward is spread abroad; so that we need not to speak any thing" (1 Thessalonians 1:7-8).

2. *You must live a life of prayer.* Combined with the Word of God is a life of prayer. Paul exemplified the heart of a true witness when he said, "Brethren, my heart's desire and prayer to God for Israel is, that they might be saved" (Romans 10:1). You should have your friends' names on your prayer list and make it a habit to daily talk to God about them. If you talk to God about your friends, it will be easy to talk to your friends about God.

Witnessing and prayer go together. In Acts 10, Peter was praying from the housetop in the city of Joppa when God told him to go and share the Gospel with Cornelius. Your success in stairstepping your friends to Christ will be directly related to the success of your prayer life.

3. *You must have biblical compassion.* You already love your friends; that is why they are your friends. But you must go beyond earthly love. Ask God to give you a heavenly love for them. The most effective motivation to stairstepping friends to Jesus Christ is the love of God in your heart. Paul had a deep love for the unsaved Jews in his day when he testified, "I have great heaviness and continual sorrow in my heart" (Romans 9:2). Paul's love

became a burden that motivated him to witness to them. Paul testifies, "For the love of Christ constraineth us; because we thus judge, that if one died for all, then were all dead" (2 Corinthians 5:14). This love motivated Paul (through hardships such as shipwrecks, beatings, and other physical abuse) to share the Gospel with lost people. Unless you have that compassion for your friends, you will not take the initiative to stairstep them to salvation.

Love will give you an urgency to share the Gospel with your friends. You do not know when your friend will die; neither do you know when you will lose every opportunity to influence them for the kingdom. The Bible says, "Behold, now is the accepted time; behold, now is the day of salvation" (2 Corinthians 6:2).

Love for your friends should motivate you to get them saved. You can't manufacture this love for your friends. It grows naturally as you pray for them and comes to full maturity as you share Christ with them. Many Christians would rather give money for a building project or do some other work for a revival crusade. They are reluctant to speak to their unchurched friends about Jesus Christ. But you must take the initiative to share the Gospel with your friends, even if it involves sacrifice.

When you love your friends, you sense their feelings. You should recognize their "seasons of the soul," times when their hearts are most tender to God. At such times a decision for Christ may be imminent. Be ready at these times to share Jesus Christ with your friends.

4. *You must listen.* The phrase "win a hearing" means you have established the right to share the Gospel with your friends. Before you can get them to listen to you, you must listen to them. Listening is the cement that holds the bricks of friendship together. Many things in your life clamor to be heard. Often these things intrude into the privacy of your home. As a result, you have the ability to tune out commercials, uninteresting conversations, and sometimes even your friends. So it is important for you to listen to them if you expect them to listen to you. When you want to introduce Jesus Christ to them, begin by being a good listener. After you have listened to what is important to them, then you can share the things that are important to you. Getting

your friends to listen to you is one step in the stairstepping process.

5. *You must be considerate.* Love is giving of yourself to your friends (see John 15:13, 1 John 3:16, 1 John 4:10). Consideration for them comes out of love, but is not the same as love. When you are considerate of your friends, you will follow the rules of courtesy in dealing with them. You will avoid offensive presentations of the Gospel that get them mad at you and turn them off to Christ and the church. If you are truly interested in your friends, you will slowly stairstep them so that they will receive you and your message. Friend Day is a good day to show friendship. On that day Christians go out of their way to take friends to church, knowing that they will hear the Gospel. If you will establish a wholesome relationship with your friends, Friend Day can be a meaningful experience.

You must earn the right to share the Gospel with your friends. When you are sensitive to them and interested in their needs, you earn the right to share the things that concern you. You earn the right to stairstep them to Christ by showing them that you really care about them. Too often unsaved friends think Christians only care about getting them to join the church or help them win an attendance contest. Your consideration is a realistic expression of your love.

6. *You must respect your friends' religious views.* The very nature of friendship is relationship. You accept your friends and respect them, and you want them to respect you in turn. The greatest attitude that you can have to tear down barriers your friends have toward Christ is to respect them where they are in life. When you accept them for what they are, you gain their confidence. To respect their religious views does not mean you agree with them. The first step to respecting your friends is to not argue with them. You can win an argument but lose a friend. And even if you win an argument, it doesn't get them saved. The second step is to recognize their right to their beliefs and their ability to reason about things. Your friend is smarter than you think. If he has wrong beliefs, he has come to them because of faulty thought processes or faulty facts. Talk with him to find out what the reasons

are for his views on religion and speak to these facts. The third step involves letting them tell you why they hold their beliefs. If you expect them to listen to you, let them explain themselves.

7. *You must be tactful.* Some Christians bluster and are offensive in pushing salvation on their friends. Tact is needed. Tact is the mental ability to do and say the right thing at the right time so as not to unjustly offend or anger. However, the Gospel will offend some, but it must still be proclaimed. At the same time, you should be careful not to use offensive methods or become offensive in your attitude. If there is any offense, let it be with the message, not in the method that you use. Jesus used tact in reaching the woman of Samaria at the well. He began at the natural point of interest, "Give me to drink" (John 4:7). He used this request to open the door of conversation with the woman. Only after he established a conversation did he mention her sinful life and point her to salvation.

In summary, stairstepping involves tact. You move your friends closer to the Gospel, yet you do not destroy your relationship with them. You can be bold, yet tactful, and by so doing you can draw them into a discussion of salvation.

8. *You must move from attitude to actions.* To win your friends to Christ involves more than being a good example. Witnessing is a definite, purposeful sharing of your Christian faith. But it doesn't always involve bringing people to a decision. Stairstepping is a deliberate effort to share the Gospel with your friends so that they may take the next step closer to Christ.

This means that you must take the initiative to bring up a conversation about Jesus Christ or your faith. Usually sinful nature and temptations from Satan will not allow a person to take a step that would bring him closer to God. Since circumstances usually will not bring about a conversation about Christ, you must be alert to your friends' immediate needs. Look for opportunities to share the Gospel with them, and take the initiative to stairstep them closer to God.

Sometimes, you will have to take a direct approach: "I would like to talk to you about becoming a Christian." Maybe that will be all that is necessary to give your friends an opportunity to express their desire for salvation. At other times you might ask, "May we talk about the Christian faith?"

9. *You must be bold without being belligerent.* Many times you may feel like Jeremiah, who said, "Ah, Lord God! behold, I cannot speak: for I am a child" (Jeremiah 1:6). You may feel that you do not have the necessary boldness to speak of Jesus Christ; therefore, you keep silent. But God gave Jeremiah a promise that applies to you. "Be not afraid of their faces: for I am with thee to deliver thee, saith the Lord" (Jeremiah 1:8). With God helping you, you will have boldness to talk about Jesus Christ. The Christian should be humble, for he knows his sinful nature, yet that should not cause him to be fearful. You should not surrender your right to talk to your friends just because you are fearful of their reaction: "For God hath not given us the spirit of fear; but of power, and of love, and of a sound mind" (2 Timothy 1:7).

Ask God for the necessary boldness to speak to your friends about Jesus Christ. The early church prayed for boldness: "Lord, behold their threatenings: and grant unto thy servants, that with all boldness they may speak thy word" (Acts 4:29). When you remember that your friends' eternal destiny may hinge on your witnessing, you will gain boldness to stairstep them to Christ. The early church received an answer to their prayer: "And with great power gave the apostles witness of the resurrection of the Lord Jesus: and great grace was upon them all" (Acts 4:33). The boldness and power that was available to the early church is available to you to witness to your friends today.

CONCLUSION

Stairstepping is not something one naturally does. It is a purposeful and intentional effort to move your friends closer to a salvation decision. Before you act, you should have the right attitude. This involves being the right kind of person and having the right equipment. Right attitudes plus right actions will lead to success in stairstepping your friends to Christ.

CHAPTER THREE

EFFECTIVE STAIRSTEPPING METHODS

You use a lever when you are trying to lift a heavy object because your power is intensified through leverage. Many of your friends may be secular and turned off to God. They will not attend church, watch Christian television, listen to Christian radio, nor read a Gospel tract. The best avenue to reach them for Christ is through your relationship with them. They know you and like you. You are a Christian and know Jesus Christ. You can introduce them to each other. Your relationship becomes a lever that can pull them toward God, like the leverage of a hammer used to pry a nail from wood.

Most of your friends live in a secular vacuum. They do not know the plan of salvation, nor do they know what they need to do to be saved. They probably know the Easter story, and they recognize a cross when they see it. They have heard the name Jesus Christ, but they do not understand the rudiments of salvation, nor do they understand spiritual maturity.

Your friends may have a bias toward God. Therefore, they may not respond to a sermon on a street corner or someone handing out Gospel literature at the airport. Your friends are most reachable through their relationship with you.

Many Christians have unsaved friends who have not become Christians, nor do they get saved when they attend church. You must use your relationship to stairstep them to salvation. But be aware that if they feel you are trying to sell them a product, like some friends use their relationship to sell encyclopedias, they will feel manipulated. The level of honesty in your relationship will determine your effectiveness in reaching them for Jesus Christ.

There are many reasons why stairstepping is effective. On the surface it seems simple, one friend talking to another about his faith. But beneath the surface, many powerful forces are at work, like the growth force of a seed that has fallen into a crack in the sidewalk and pushes heavy concrete out of the way. Stairstepping can be effective if the following methods are used:

1. *Use existing networks.* Sometimes it is difficult to go out and make friends with unsaved people, especially if the purpose is to win them to Christ. When people become Christians, they separate themselves from the world, including profane language, off-color jokes, slurs, and immoral practices. These new Christians are uncomfortable with the unsaved because they want to keep themselves holy. Most would rather fellowship with other Christians because of their mutual love for Jesus Christ and their mutual value systems.

However, Christians network into a world of both saved and unsaved people. They go on coffee breaks with both at work, and their children play little league ball together. Therefore, using existing relationships with the unsaved is an excellent way to begin stairstepping them to Christ. On some occasions, Christians will have to make new relationships with the unsaved. Christians cannot isolate themselves in this world; they are to be ambassadors for Jesus Christ.

2. *Win a hearing.* Before you can win your friends to Christ, you must win them to you. This is the source of the term "Friendship Evangelism." You use your friendship for three steps toward salvation. In the first step, your friends are won to you. In the second step, they are won to the fellowship of the church, and third, they are won to Christ.

Since you already have relationships with unsaved people, you need to build on those networks, which are like a spider's web. Just as a spider catches things in its web, you need to incorporate your friends into your thinking, your struggles, and then into your Christian faith. Because of your friends' secular nature, they need to see Jesus Christ in your life. They may be blinded to spiritual truth, and religious words may not affect them. Sermons may roll off them like water beads off a formica cabinet top, but your relationship to them does three things. First, it puts flesh on abstract religious words. The words *grace, sin,* and *conversion* mean nothing to them until they see them in your life.

Second, your friends may reject the historical Jesus because of their preconceptions, but they can see Jesus in you: "Christ in you, the hope of glory" (Colossians 1:27). In your networking relationship, you communicate apart from words. You communicate heart-to-heart. Your friends identify with "Christ in you" and desire to be like Him. Your relationship becomes the avenue for motivating them to conversion.

Finally, your lifestyle becomes an example for them. They will look up to some strength in you and desire to be like you. Because Christ is the source of your joy, they will want to become Christians. Before your friends hear the Gospel from your lips, you must establish credibility by your testimony. This is "winning a hearing." This means that your lifestyle actually wins them to you, not that you are the most important thing, but they see Jesus Christ in your values and attitudes.

You "win a hearing" when you demonstrate that Jesus Christ is meeting the needs of your life (see 2 Corinthians 9:8). If you are not victorious, it will be difficult to convince your friends that such a victory is available to them. But this does not mean that you are perfect. Be open and transparent with your friends; allow them to see your problems and also your burdens. Show them how God helps you through your problems. Do not try to convince them that you are perfect, just show them that you are a struggling sinner. Your friends will identify with your struggles, as well as with your victories.

3. *Share from your strength.* Since the Christian knows Christ, he becomes the bridge over which his friends travel to salvation. Part of the definition of evangelism is communicating the Gospel to someone at their point of need. Communicate actually means "to have in common." Friends have things in common and they communicate. Communicate your love, peace, and joy to your friends.

God communicated with man in many ways, but the greatest was through Jesus Christ. Christianity is a relationship between God and man. It is based on the life, death, and resurrection of Jesus Christ. When you become a Christian, you become a child of God and have a living relationship with Him.

The basis of your friend's communication with God is the Gospel. They cannot get saved apart from the Gospel. Some think the Gospel is something to know, but it is more than that because knowledge never saved anyone. There is a propositional Gospel and a personal Gospel. The propositional Gospel is the good news of the death, burial, and resurrection of Jesus Christ. A person must know these facts to be saved. Paul explains, "I declare unto you the gospel which I preached unto you, . . . how that Christ died for our sins according to the scriptures; And that he was buried, and that he rose again the third day according to the scriptures" (1 Corinthians 15:1, 3-4). However, knowing the propositional Gospel has not saved anyone.

The Gospel is a person; the Gospel is Jesus Christ. When your friends give mental assent to the propositional Gospel, they have taken a step closer to salvation. Now they must know Jesus Christ as Savior. They must pray and ask Jesus Christ to come into their heart: "But as many as received him, to them gave he power to become the sons of God" (John 1:12). By definition *evangelism* is the communication of the Gospel in an understandable manner, motivating a person to respond to Christ and become a member of His church.

4. *Reach the reachable.* For many years the church zeroed in on prospects in evangelism. A prospect was considered any person in the immediate vicinity of the church who was not already a member of that church nor a member of another church. Prospects were reached by canvasing door-to-door, passing out literature, or preaching over radio or television. But many prospects were not reachable. Since it is never known who is most reachable in any neighborhood, the church must continue saturation evangelism, that is, "using every available means to reach every available person at every available time." By this method, some are moved from nonreceptivity and become receptive people.

However, because of limited budgets, limited workers, and the continuing need to evangelize, the church should focus its outreach in the community on the people who are the most receptive to Christ. Those who are the most receptive are your friends.

Since the church should focus on those who are the most receptive, a Friend Day or other form of friendship evangelism is probably the most effective form of outreach. Jesus compared evangelism to sowing seed in different types of soil. In Matthew 13:3-23, the seed is the Word of God, and the soil is people's hearts. Jesus described the wayside soil as hardened people who were unreceptive to the Gospel. After they heard the message they rejected it. Then He described the stony soil as people who superficially heard the message. The seed sprouted up quickly, but because it had no depth of earth, it died under the scorching sun. The third type of soil was thorny soil. These people temporarily received the Gospel, but were unwilling to make the changes required of them. Therefore, their receptivity was temporary. Finally, the truly receptive people were called good ground. They responded to the Gospel and became fruitful.

The degree of receptivity to the Gospel will vary from one of your friends to the next. Your closest friend may not be as open to the Gospel as a casual acquaintance. Receptivity not only varies from person to person but also from time to time. Your friends change with the passage of time and events. Someone who is unreceptive today may become very open to the Gospel tomorrow. Therefore, when you share Jesus Christ with them, you have planted a seed. Just as it takes time for a seed to grow to maturity, so it takes time to stairstep a friend to Christ. Do not expect immediate results. Just as a farmer must have patience to wait for the seed to break through the soil, you must have patience in stairstepping your friends to Christ.

5. *Watch for seasons of the soul.* Just as there is a season to plant and a season to harvest, so there are seasons in the lives of your friends when they are "ripe to harvest." The phrase "seasons of the soul" describes a time when your friends are responsive to the Gospel. This is also described as being receptive. They are receptive to you and responsive to your message.

Supernatural influences make your friends receptive-responsive people. First, there is the conviction of the Holy Spirit, whereby they see their sin and its result in their life. Since the Holy Spirit brings conviction through the Word of God, the degree of receptivity may be directly related to the amount of Bible teaching they have heard and understood. Second, your godly testimony or the lifestyle of another Christian can bring conviction. Third, God speaks to them through nature or their contacts with the church and Christians.

But natural factors also make your friends receptive to Jesus Christ. These are internal disequilibriums or disruptive events that shake their security. In a crisis or a disappointment, your friend may be unsettled and turn to God. Such crises may be being fired, declaring bankruptcy, going to jail, experiencing a long-term illness or a death in the family, or any event that shakes their complacency and shocks their system.

In addition, positive events may prepare your friends to listen to the Gospel. These are also "seasons of the soul." Examples are marriage, the birth of a child, promotion, or even being transferred and moving from one community to another. At these times, many people change their values and their perspective. Because they are changing, they are open to the Gospel.

For example, when a person moves from one home to another, especially if he moves far away, his family and lifestyle are disrupted. In this moment of transition, he can be reached with the Gospel. Watch for these signs of openness in your friends.

6. *Be aware that receptivity extends to both the messenger and the message.* Your friends may possibly reject the message of Jesus Christ, but may not reject you. On the other hand, some people turn off the messenger, but they do not have any hatred toward God. Jesus warned about this two-fold possibility when He told his disciples, "And whosoever shall not receive you, nor hear your words, when ye depart out of that house or city, shake off the dust of your feet" (Matthew 10:14). The words *receive* and *hear* in this verse mean "to approve" and "to give ear." The two possible rejections were that the unsaved would reject the messenger, or they would refuse to listen to the message. However, the fact that you have a networking relationship with your friend means that they have not rejected you, the messenger. Therefore, use your relationship for effective evangelism.

The rich young ruler apparently had confidence in Jesus. He came, fell at Jesus' feet, and addressed him as "Good Master," which literally means, "good teacher." The word *good* means "honorable or acceptable." The rich young ruler appeared to be receptive to Jesus. However, when Jesus questioned him concerning his total commitment, the young ruler was not willing to give up his riches (see Matthew 19:16-22). He was receptive to the messenger but rejected the message. Likewise, some of your friends will listen to you, but will reject the Gospel message.

7. *Recognize barriers.* Some people will not receive Christ because of barriers they see in your life, your church, or in Christianity in general. Some barriers are real (a Christian has offended them), and some barriers are imagined (they are fearful of being embarrassed in a Gospel church service). Some barriers are natural, and you can do nothing about them. For instance, the message of repentance found in Acts 2:38 is a barrier to those who do not want to give up their sin. This first barrier may involve something they do, some place they go, or some relationship they have difficulty giving up. Second, the message of the cross is a barrier to some. They either consider the cross foolish (see 1 Corinthians 1:18), or they take offense at its message (see Galatians 5:11). In the third place, some people work for salvation, and the message of grace is a barrier. But the Bible teaches, "For by grace are ye saved through faith; and that not of yourselves: it is the gift of God: Not of works . . ." (Ephesians 2:8, 9). These are all barriers that you cannot remove.

Some of your friends have barriers created by prejudice or wrong interpretations. In the early 1960s along Highway 301 in central Florida, there was an American buffalo ranch that was open to the public. The massive buffalo were restrained by only a flimsy chicken wire fence. When the attendant was asked about the security of the fence, he indicated that the buffalo could run right through any fence that was put up, so a chicken wire fence was as good as a steel fence. The attendant explained, "When they see the fence, they think that they can't get through." The chicken wire fence was primarily a mental barrier. Most of the barriers our friends have are mental barriers.

Barriers are built both by believers and the non-churched. Christians build barriers from inside the church. They fear being contaminated by the influence of worldly people or being embarrassed by their practices. They are also ashamed of their own inability to develop meaningful relationships with the unsaved.

Your unsaved friends build barriers from the outside. They fear what they do not understand. Sometimes they feel convicted in the presence of the people of God. Sometimes the barrier is caused by ignorance. They do not understand the church, its language, or its music. When they come in through the front door, they fear that they will be asked to sign something, sing, stand up, or say something. Paul indicated that the unsaved man does not understand the things of God, nor the people of God (see 1 Corinthians 2:14-15). Therefore, unsaved people are more comfortable remaining outside the church and its stained glass barriers.

Sometimes Christians create barriers by their judgmental attitudes. The unsaved person looks at the Christian's list of acceptable and unacceptable behavior and sees that they fall short. (For example, they may take the name of God in vain, smoke, or drink.) As a result they find themselves either defending their actions or being convicted of their lifestyle.

Legalism and traditions of men are barriers. When your friends come into the church, they either apologize for their actions or are irritated by the judgmental attitude of Christians. Rather than being attracted to Jesus Christ, legalism drives your friends away. Remember, the law may bring conviction of sin, but the law never saves. When the law is wrongly presented, it becomes a legalistic barrier to the Gospel.

8. *Overcome barriers.* Most barriers to reaching your friends for Christ are as easily overcome as the chicken wire fence used to restrain buffalo in Florida. However, the barriers remain because they are perceived to be barriers. You may not be responsible for erecting them, but you must overcome them if you will reach your friends for Christ.

Just as a doctor must diagnose an illness before he can begin to treat it, the first step in removing barriers is to recognize them.

Paul said, "I am made all things to all men, that I might by all means save some" (1 Corinthians 9:22).

Do not let your fear of sharing Christ be a barrier. Paul had a very real problem with fear. He wrote to the church at Corinth, "I was with you in weakness, and in fear, and in much trembling" (1 Corinthians 2:3). Even though fear was an apparent barrier to him, he asked the Ephesians to pray for him that he might share the Gospel without fear (see Ephesians 6:19).

Christians also fear being infected with sin. Jesus prayed for Christians that they should not be taken out of the world (isolated), but that they should be guarded (insulated) against it. His petition was, "That thou shouldest keep them from the evil" (John 17:15).

Once a Christian overcomes his fear, he simply opens up and talks freely about his faith in Jesus Christ. Make an appointment with your friends. Take them to lunch and commit yourself by saying, "There is something I need to talk to you about." Once you make the commitment, share your faith boldly.

CONCLUSION

Stairstepping is more than inviting a friend to church or preaching to them. There are powerful forces at work as you attempt to influence them. You must recognize the reciprocity of networking. There are many things that you share with your friends. Make sure you share all of your life; tell them about your faith. You can't reach everyone in your neighborhood, but you are expected to reach the reachable, your friends. There will be times when they are open to the Gospel. This is called "seasons of the soul." Also, there are degrees of receptivity to you and responsiveness to the Gospel. Timing is important. Know how to recognize and remove barriers to the Gospel in the lives of your friends. Knowledge of these factors in stairstepping your friends to Christ will help you be more successful.

CHAPTER FOUR

HOW TO INVITE YOUR FRIENDS TO CHURCH

Most Christians have friends who are unsaved. They know it is their duty to win non-Christians to Christ, but Christians usually don't know how to do it; or if they know how, they are afraid to do it. For any one of many reasons, Christians just don't seem to be winning their unsaved friends to Christ.

There is one thing that Christians can do to get their friends saved. They can invite them to attend church with them where the Word of God is preached. However, just attending worship services will never get anyone saved. But if your unsaved friends are properly prepared before they visit the church and proper follow-up is done, there is a better chance of them getting saved.

Some unsaved people attend church, with or without friends, where they are then converted. But the vast majority of those who visit the typical Sunday morning church service do not get saved. Why? Because attending church is not part of the stairstepping process.

IS INVITING EVANGELISM BIBLICAL?

The phrase "Front Door Evangelism" is used to describe outreach to unsaved people who visit a church and hear the good news of Jesus' death, burial, and resurrection. This is a descriptive term used to communicate the avenue that people follow to hear the Gospel and become converted.

"Front Door Evangelism" is also called "Inviting Evangelism" because both friends and strangers are attracted to the church through invitation. You invite your friends to hear your pastor or attend your church. Sometimes Inviting Evangelism takes place by impersonal means, such as a letter, flyer, poster, or some form of mass media.

Some have suggested that because the terms Inviting Evangelism and Front Door Evangelism are not found in the pages of

Scripture, they are wrong and a nonbiblical expression of evangelism.

But because these terms are not found in the Bible in the form in which they are used in contemporary churches does not mean that they are wrong. One leading pastor once said, "Most will only do what is biblical to win the lost. But because I love the lost, I'll go a step further. I'll do anything that is not nonbiblical."

The following points give biblical foundation to Inviting Evangelism.

1. *Lost people attended New Testament church services.* There were occasions when unsaved people attended the services in the New Testament. When Paul discussed the problem of the expression of miraculous gifts during the church service, he noted, "If therefore the whole church be come together into one place, and all speak with tongues, and there come in those that are unlearned, or unbelievers, will they not say that ye are mad?" (1 Corinthians 14:23) Paul was dealing with the abuses of tongues, and noted that when tongues were wrongly used, there were no conversions. The abuse was a barrier to the unsaved who attended the worship services. The passage shows that unsaved people attended the services of Christians.

Further reinforcement of this view is found in Paul's statement that "tongues are for a sign, not to them that believe, but to them that believe not" (1 Corinthians 14:22). This meant that before the authority of the Word of God was fully established, tongues was the authority that made the unsaved listen with responsive hearts to the revelation of God. Since Paul was dealing with the expression of tongues in the assembly, by application he was saying the unsaved attended their services.

An illustration in James 2:1-7 also suggests that unsaved people visited believer's services. Christians apparently were outwardly impressed with rich people who visited their assembly, giving them the best seats: "For if there come unto your assembly a man with a gold ring, in goodly apparel . . . ye have respect to him . . . and say unto him, sit thou here in a good place" (James 2:2-3). This may have been a reference to rich Christians, but was probably not. James suggested that these rich men were not their friends: "Do not rich men oppress you, and draw you before the judgment seats? Do not they blaspheme that worthy name by the which ye are called" (James 2:6-7). James was not suggesting that unsaved rich people not attend church, but that when they came into the assembly, they should be treated equally like the poor.

2. *The lost heard preaching.* The New Testament described preaching on the street corner, in the marketplace, and in the synagogue. These locations were where (1) the public gathered, (2) public messages were announced, and (3) communication within the community took place. At times it appeared that both preaching and teaching occurred in these public places.

Paul went into the synagogue to preach in Antioch (Acts 13:14), Iconium (Acts 14:1), Thessalonica (Acts 17:1), Berea (Acts 17:10), and Corinth (Acts 18:1). The synagogue (which comes from the words *together* and *to teach*) was not primarily a place of Jewish worship, but was more like a Jewish convention center because those of every Jewish sect had access to it for teaching, discussing, or communicating. Some considered Christianity a Jewish sect, so Paul had access to the synagogue in each city until he was driven out because of his message.

The early church met in synagogues, and the non-Christian Jewish community attended. Many unsaved people came to hear the message, both Jews and Gentiles (Acts 18:4). That means that Front Door Evangelism was operative.

3. *The command to "go preach" suggests Front Door Evangelism.* Jesus gave the command, "Go ye into all the world, and preach the gospel to every creature" (Mark 16:15). The church is to preach the Gospel to lost people. This is done when Christians go out and present the plan of salvation to the lost, but it is also accomplished when Christians get unsaved people to come into their preaching services through Front Door Evangelism or Inviting Evangelism.

STEPS TO INVITING EVANGELISM

1. *Be convinced of your strategy.* Be positive when you talk to your friends about Christ and your church. Your friends know you, and they will recognize your tension or guilt if you have a hidden agenda when you talk to them. You develop hidden agendas when you feel guilty for not talking to your friends about Christ. You feel guilty especially if you sit under preaching that constantly condemns you for not being a soul-winner. Remember, you are not inviting your friends to church to get rid of guilt. If you have a negative motivation, it will surface and become a barrier to reaching them. You can't fool your friends.

When you invite friends to church, you must be convinced that it is part of a strategy that will ultimately change their life. What will give you this positive attitude? First, you must have a conviction that Inviting Evangelism is biblical. Second, you must believe that what you are doing will lead to the salvation of your friends.

2. *Be sure of your relationship.* Friends love because they want to, not because they must. And because they love, they want to share. This means sharing experiences, thoughts, opinions, and activities.

At this point you can stairstep your friends to salvation by letting them know that your faith is important to you and that you are fulfilled through your experiences at church. When your friends see how important your church is to you, they will be willing to listen to you. Why? Because friendship is sharing each other's lives.

3. *Explain your motives.* You want your friends to go to church with you, but they may have some wrong ideas about church attendance. Your friends may think you are trying to sell them something. Sometimes friends are invited to a party where they are given a pitch to buy plastic kitchenware or aluminum pots. Because some abuse their friendships, your friends may think you want them to "buy," so they resist going to church with you or they put you off.

On occasion people have invited their friends to church to win a prize, to pack a pew, or to break an attendance record. You may be able to do this effectively, but always keep your motives aboveboard. Otherwise, your friends may feel used or manipulated. Explain to them that you want them to know what you believe and why you believe it. You want them to understand why your faith is meaningful to you.

When your church has a Friend Day, explain that everyone is bringing a friend and you want them to come as your friend. Explain that there will be things that friends do together on Friend Day. The sermon that day will probably emphasize friendship and the two of you can enjoy it together.

4. *Raise and answer questions before they do.* If they have barriers in their mind against attending your church and they never voice them, they may politely refuse and never attend. You will not be able to overcome these barriers if you don't know about them. If they raise questions about problems in your church, you are placed on the defensive. When you are on the defensive, it is difficult to be positive. Therefore, mention possible barriers before they raise them.

Research indicates that the unsaved have four fears about attending church. They fear they will be asked:

1. To stand up in a crowd

2. To speak up in a crowd

3. To sign something

4. To give money

In some churches visitors are asked to stand and introduce themselves, a practice that is embarrassing to some people. Perhaps a talk with the pastor will help. If he insists, you might arrange for your friends to be excluded. Then tell your friends that they won't be publicly identified.

Let your friends know exactly what will happen to them when they attend your church. They should know whether everyone repeats the Lord's Prayer or reads the responsive reading. If your worship service has any other unique features, explain them to your friend before entering the church. If they are at ease, they will get more out of the service and may respond to the invitation.

5. *Build up anticipation.* Tell them about the things you enjoy, such as praise choruses, Bible exposition, or sharing time. Since they are your friends, they will want to enjoy what you enjoy. But do more than point out what you enjoy, tell them why. This is a good opportunity to share a testimony of what Christ has done for you and how He did it.

In Step 4, you openly discussed any barriers your friends might experience. Now that you've eliminated the negative, you must emphasize the positive. Put a little salt on their tongues so they will be thirsty for Jesus Christ.

A BIBLICAL EXAMPLE OF EFFECTIVE STAIRSTEPPING

Cornelius, a Roman army officer, was an honest seeker of salvation. He prayed daily and did good works, but these did not qualify him for salvation. God sent an angel to tell him to send for the Apostle Peter. (Note: An angel does not give the plan of salvation; that task is left to Christians.) Notice what Cornelius did to prepare his heart and the hearts of his friends.

1. *He gathered his family and friends.* Cornelius gathered with his friends to hear the Word of God preached. God had spoken to him and he wanted others to hear the message. Several words are used to describe the group that Cornelius gathered to hear the message. He "called together his kinsmen and near friends" (Acts 10:24). God promised Cornelius that Peter would preach a message: "whereby thou, and all thy house shall be saved" (Acts 11:14).

2. *They came ready to listen.* Cornelius indicated that they were not only present, but were prepared "to hear all things that are commanded thee of God" (Acts 10:33). Cornelius had stairstepped them so that they were ready for God's Word. This shows their anticipation.

3. *They were ready to get saved.* The task was properly done. Cornelius' family and friends were properly conditioned and ready to be saved. The messengers told Peter that Cornelius had sent "to hear words of thee" (Acts 10:22). When you properly stairstep your friends, they are likely to get saved when they attend church.

CONCLUSION

It is biblical to invite your friends to church where they can hear the Gospel and get saved. There are several instances of unsaved people attending preaching services in the New Testament. However, just because your friends attend church with you does not mean that they will get saved. But if you properly prepare them to receive the message, there is a greater likelihood that they will. Cornelius properly prepared his friends to hear Peter's message. As a result, they were converted.

APPENDIX A

HOW TO LEAD YOUR FRIENDS TO CHRIST

Not everyone knows how to lead friends to Christ, but anyone can learn. I use the following steps constantly. As a matter of fact, week by week in the counseling room in my church, I usually follow the same procedure to lead people to Christ. My approach is not set in concrete, nor is it mechanical. It is meaningful to me because it gives me direction in talking to people about Christ. When you talk with your friends, be careful not to offend them or force your decision upon them. If they make a decision just to please you, they will not be saved; and if they pray just because you ask them, they will not be converted. The decision to trust Christ must come from their heart, and they must pray sincerely when they trust Him for salvation.

THE ROMAN ROAD OF SALVATION

The Bible uses the illustration of a road to picture conversion: "Enter ye in at the strait gate: for wide is the gate, and broad is the way, that leadeth to destruction, and many there be which go in thereat: Because strait is the gate, and narrow is the way, which leadeth unto life . . ." (Matthew 7:13-14). Jesus also used this analogy when he said, "I am the way, the truth, and the life: no man cometh unto the Father, but by me" (John 14:6). When someone trusts Jesus Christ, they get on the road to the Heavenly Father. In the book of Acts, early Christianity was referred to as "the way" (Acts 9:2).

The phrase "the Roman Road of Salvation" is used to describe the salvation verses found in the book of Romans. Just as in Bible times travelers followed Roman roads to get to their destination, so today a person can walk through several verses in the book of Romans to learn truth that will lead to salvation. Many other verses could be used in leading people to Jesus Christ. However, I use the Roman Road for a couple of reasons. First, these verses are familiar to me and I am comfortable using them. The Roman Road is like a tool, and carpenters go back to the tool they use most effectively to get the job done. Also, I prefer to use a few verses in one book when talking to an unsaved person. If the seeker must constantly shift his attention from one Bible book to another and read a multitude of verses, he is likely to become confused. Therefore, I take a few verses and explain them well rather than using many verses. I slowly explain each verse so the person is more likely to see God's plan of salvation. You might want to underline these verses in your Bible with a pen. Then when a friend is reading the plan of salvation, they will stand out on the page.

THE ROMAN ROAD OF SALVATION

Romans 3:23 = Man's Need

Romans 6:23 = Sin's Penalty

Romans 5:8 = God's Provision

Romans 10:9 = Man's Response

GETTING STARTED

Many Christians do not share their faith because they do not know how to get started. I suggest that you begin by sharing your testimony with your unsaved friends. In a testimony, simply share how you came to Jesus Christ. The words *testimony* and *sharing* also mean witnessing: "Ye shall be witnesses unto me" (Acts 1:8). When a Christian witnesses, he simply tells what God has done for him, which is telling what he has seen, heard, and experienced.

In the early church, Peter and John testified, " We cannot but speak the things which we have seen and heard" (Acts 4:20). They did not preach a sermon, nor did they give out Gospel literature. They simply shared what they had seen and heard.

Later the healed man came before the Sanhedrin. He did not give a verbal testimony, but his changed life gave a silent testimony. The Sanhedrin was moved by this: "And beholding the man which was healed standing with them, they could say nothing against it" (Acts 4:14).

When you give a testimony for Jesus Christ, simply tell what He means to you. Your testimony should answer the following three questions:

1. What was your life like before conversion?

2. How did you receive Christ?

3. What does Christ mean to you now?

Maybe you cannot remember the exact date you were saved. Perhaps you were converted early in life. If you cannot share the events of your conversion experience, you can share the present reality of your Christian walk. After you have shared your testimony with a friend, ask one of the following questions:

1. What is your reaction to that?

2. Would you like to know Jesus Christ?

3. May I show you from the Bible how you can receive Jesus Christ?

Questions are like a scalpel in the surgeon's hand; questions cut and open to get at a problem. When you ask your friends one of these questions, they will respond in different ways. Most will not want to get on their knees and pray to receive Christ immediately. They will say things like: ". . .Oh." and that's all they will say, or "That's nice. . ." Again they'll not say "Yes" or "No," but "I'll have to think about that."

Most of your friends will not get converted simply because you share Christ with them. But by sharing Christ you have stairstepped them closer to salvation. Even though they do not get saved at that moment, they will think about what you have said. If you have prayed and committed your witness to Jesus Christ, the Holy Spirit will work in their hearts. Therefore, do not try to press a decision on them at this point unless they are interested. If they are not interested, continue to share your witness or answer any questions they may raise. Let them know what God has done for you through your church. Tell them what you get out of hymn singing, worship, or Bible study. Perhaps you will be able to persuade them to attend church with you where they can hear the Gospel.

WALKING THE ROMAN ROAD

Some of those to whom you witness will ask questions; others will let you explain the plan of salvation. Therefore, turn in your Bible to Romans 3:23 and make sure that they can read the text for themselves as you read it aloud.

Man's Need

For all have sinned, and come short of the glory of God.
Romans 3:23

Explain that the word *all* includes everyone in the world, you as well as them. Quickly clarify that you are not preaching to them, but you are identifying them with this verse. Point out that every Christian is a sinner. Even though a Christian is saved by grace, he is a sinner saved by grace.

The word *sin* does not mean that your friends are hopeless social outcasts. It means they have fallen short of God's standard. They have not prayed as often or as much as they should. Your friends are not as perfect as Jesus Christ, who perfectly obeyed the law of God. If your friends have broken one spiritual law, they are guilty of breaking all God's laws (James 2:10). Don't preach to your friends, just explain how God looks at people; imperfect people are sinners. If your friends will not accept the fact that they are sinners, it may be useless to continue to explain the Roman Road of Salvation. A wise teacher once told me, "You can't get people converted until you get them lost." By this he explained that people must be convinced of their need for salvation before they will truly seek the Lord Jesus Christ. It's like the old farmer said, "Until you get them thirsty, they won't drink." After they are convinced that they have sinned and come short of the glory of God, move on to the penalty for sin.

Sin's Penalty

For the wages of sin is death; but the gift of God is eternal life through Jesus Christ our Lord.
Romans 6:23

Remind your friends that the word *wages* is what they are paid by their employer for the work they have done. Wages in the average person's vocabulary is money they have coming to them at the end of the week. When they work for a week, they will get a paycheck. In God's sight those who have sinned will get their paycheck; it is death. The wages of sin is death.

Next, point to the word *gift* and contrast a gift and wages. A gift is free; it is something you don't deserve. You work for wages and get what you deserve. Explain to your friends that they do not deserve eternal life, yet God promises to give them eternal life through Jesus Christ.

You don't give gifts to your enemies or strangers. You give gifts to people you know or love. God knows you and has given you a gift because He loves you. That gift is eternal life through the Lord Jesus Christ.

Turn to Romans 5:8 and point out the words *sinners* and *died*.

God's Provision

But God commendeth his love toward us, in that, while we were yet sinners, Christ died for us.
Romans 5:8

Jesus Christ died for sinners (you and your friends). This is the Gospel, which is good news. The bad news is that "the wages of sin is death." But your friends don't have to go to hell; they can have eternal life. That's good news. Your friends should have been punished, but Christ took their punishment.

Tell your friends the story of Easter, how Christ died upon a cross. It was not just a martyr's death; Christ died as a substitute for your friends. Then point out that Christ was buried and on the third day He rose again. In the Resurrection, Christ has eternal life that He now gives to those who believe on Him. Your friends probably understand the events that surround Easter, but now you must explain the meaning of these events to them.

The word *commendeth* means to give. God commended or gave His love to us rather than giving us the wages of sin. The last step in the Roman Road is your friends' response. Turn to Romans 10:9, and explain that mere knowledge of the death of Christ will not get them to heaven. After your friends know that Christ has died for them, they must respond in faith.

Man's Response

That if thou shalt confess with thy mouth the Lord Jesus, and shalt believe in thine heart that God hath raised him from the dead, thou shalt be saved.
Romans 10:9

There are many people who know intellectually about Jesus Christ. They can even say, "Jesus died for me." But knowledge of Christ's death will not convert anyone. Your friends must do more than know; they must respond. Your friends must now make a decision. They must choose the narrow road to salvation or the broad road that leads to destruction. Point out that only they can make that choice. You cannot do it for them, neither can their spouse or parents. It is a commitment they must make themselves. The word *heart* explains the personality or the inner self of your friends. They must believe with all their heart and accept Christ as Savior. Many misunderstand the word *believe* and do not have saving belief. The word *believe* can mean speculation, such as "I believe next year we will show a profit in our business," or "I believe it is going to rain tomorrow." In some instances, the word *believe* is used to mean acquaintance with facts, such as, "I believe in the historical fact of World War II." Just to believe historical facts about Jesus will not save your friends. The Bible says, "The devils also believe, and tremble" (James 2:19). Obviously, the devils are not saved.

Believing is described in the Gospel of John as drinking (John 4:14), eating (John 6:35), receiving (John 1:12), or seeing (John 3:14, Numbers 21:9). Believing involves the total person's response to God with his intellect, his emotions, and his will. The Bible uses the act of receiving Christ as a synonym of believing. "But as many as received him, to them gave he power to become the sons of God, even to them that believe on his name" (John 1:12).

POINTING TO A DECISION

After you have walked your friends through the Roman Road of Salvation, do not leave them with head knowledge. Now you must give them an opportunity to make a decision for Jesus Christ. Use the following questions to prepare them for a decision:

1. "Do you understand God's plan for salvation?"

2. "Would you like to receive Jesus Christ as your Savior?"

3. "Would you like to pray now?"

If your friends give an affirmative answer to any one of the questions, encourage them to pray with you. Some who want to be saved can pray in their own words. They simply express belief in Jesus Christ and ask for forgiveness of sins. Others will not know how to pray. Tell them, "I will lead you in a prayer. After I pray a sentence, I want you to pray that sentence out loud." At this point, begin praying and wait for them to follow your lead.

After your friends have received Christ, you might want to offer a prayer of thanksgiving. Make your prayer short and to the point. Thank God for saving them.

COMMITMENT

When your friends have prayed to receive Christ, you will want to confirm them in their faith. Turn to John 6:37. "All that the Father giveth me shall come to me; and him that cometh to me I will in no wise cast out." Ask your friends if they just came to Christ. If they say, "Yes," tell them that the Father has received them and will not cast them out. They are now Christians and must begin to grow in grace.

SUMMARY

The Roman Road of Salvation explains what a person needs to know to be saved. First, your friends must know and acknowledge that they are sinners. Second, they must recognize the penalty for their sin, which is death. Third, they must recognize that Jesus Christ has died for their sins. This is good news because Jesus has paid the price on the cross for sin. Lastly, your friends should know that they must respond to Jesus Christ by receiving Him. These simple facts are all they need to know to be saved. If they will pray sincerely from their heart, God will save them.

APPENDIX B

GLOSSARY

Arrested Spiritual Development - when a church stops growing internally (i.e., lack of prayer, sin, lack of Bible reading, and no vision), it ultimately stops growing externally. Internal growth (growth in grace) becomes the foundation of numerical growth.

Discipling - causing those who have accepted Christ to grow to maturity in their faith so that they can reach others for Christ.

E-O Evangelism - evangelism of unsaved members within the church congregation.

E-l Evangelism - evangelism that crosses barriers related to the church building or the perception of the church in the minds of the unsaved.

E-2 Evangelism - evangelism that crosses cultural and class barriers.

E-3 Evangelism - evangelism that crosses linguistic barriers.

Event Evangelism - see Front Door Evangelism.

Evangelism - communicating the Gospel to people in an understandable way and motivating people to respond to Christ and become members of His church.

Evangelist - a gifted individual whom God has given to the church to work in winning others to Christ.

Faith - the God-given ability to undertake a task for God and to sustain unwavering confidence that God will accomplish the task in spite of all obstacles.

F.R.A.N. - acrostic for friends, relatives, associates, and neighbors.

Friendship Evangelism - the principle of reaching others for Christ through natural relationships (with friends, relatives, associates, and neighbors).

Front Door Evangelism - inviting people to enter through the front door of the church where they can hear the Gospel in an event and be saved.

Maturing - bringing a person to completion or making him well-rounded.

Networking - the principle of establishing and building redemptive friendships for the purpose of evangelism.

Nurturing - see Maturing.

Reaching - making contact with a person and motivating him to give an honest hearing to the Gospel.

Receptive-Responsive People - prospects who are receptive to the messenger and responsive to the message of the Gospel.

Saturation Evangelism - using every available means to reach every available person at every available time.

Shepherding - fulfilling the threefold responsibility of (1) leading the flock, (2) feeding the flock, and (3) protecting the flock.

Side Door Evangelism - first, networking people with church members; second, networking them into the activities of the church; and third, through these relationships, networking them to Jesus Christ.

Spiritual Gift - a special ability given by the Holy Spirit to enable a Christian to serve productively in the body of Christ.

Stairstepping - a systematic and natural approach of bringing people to Christ one step at a time.

Testimony Evangelism - sharing our experience in Jesus Christ with other people so that they, too, will want to experience what we have in Christ.

Winning - communicating the Gospel in an understandable manner and motivating a person to respond.

NOTES

**IMPORTANT THINGS I'VE LEARNED
ABOUT HOW TO REACH MY FRIENDS FOR CHRIST**

NOTES

**MY PERSONAL TESTIMONY
OF WHAT CHRIST HAS DONE FOR ME**